A Visual Guide to Scales for Mandolin

Benjamin M. Taylor

Contents

Introduction 10
    The Aims of This Book 10
    Why Learn to Play Scales? 10
    How to Use This Book 10
    Using Scale Diagrams to Construct Exercises 11
    Author's Notes on this Edition 11
Root note: C 13
    C Aeolian 13
    C Algerian 13
    C Arabic 13
    C Bebop Dominant 13
    C Bebop Major 13
    C Bebop Minor 13
    C Chinese 13
    C Dorian 13
    C Egyptian 14
    C Enigmatic 14
    C Gypsy 14
    C Harmonic Minor 14
    C Hindu 14
    C Hirajoshi 14
    C Hungarian 14
    C Japanese 14
    C Locrian 15
    C Lydian 15
    C Major Blues 15
    C Major (Ionian) 15
    C Melodic Minor 15
    C Minor Blues 15
    C Mixolydian 15
    C Nine Tone 15
    C Oriental 16
    C Pentatonic Major 16
    C Pentatonic Minor 16
    C Persian 16
    C Phrygian 16
    C Romanian Minor 16
    C Spanish 8 Tone 16
    C Spanish Gypsy 16
    C Symmetric Dim. 1 17
    C Symmetric Dim. 2 17
Root note: C♯/D♭ 17
    C♯/D♭ Aeolian 17
    C♯/D♭ Algerian 17
    C♯/D♭ Arabic 17
    C♯/D♭ Bebop Dominant 17
    C♯/D♭ Bebop Major 18
    C♯/D♭ Bebop Minor 18
    C♯/D♭ Chinese 18
    C♯/D♭ Dorian 18
    C♯/D♭ Egyptian 18
    C♯/D♭ Enigmatic 18
    C♯/D♭ Gypsy 18
    C♯/D♭ Harmonic Minor 18
    C♯/D♭ Hindu 19
    C♯/D♭ Hirajoshi 19
    C♯/D♭ Hungarian 19
    C♯/D♭ Japanese 19

C♯/D♭ Locrian 19
C♯/D♭ Lydian 19
C♯/D♭ Major Blues 19
C♯/D♭ Major (Ionian) 19
C♯/D♭ Melodic Minor 20
C♯/D♭ Minor Blues 20
C♯/D♭ Mixolydian 20
C♯/D♭ Nine Tone 20
C♯/D♭ Oriental 20
C♯/D♭ Pentatonic Major 20
C♯/D♭ Pentatonic Minor 20
C♯/D♭ Persian 20
C♯/D♭ Phrygian 21
C♯/D♭ Romanian Minor 21
C♯/D♭ Spanish 8 Tone 21
C♯/D♭ Spanish Gypsy 21
C♯/D♭ Symmetric Dim. 1 21
C♯/D♭ Symmetric Dim. 2 21
Root note: D 21
    D Aeolian 22
    D Algerian 22
    D Arabic 22
    D Bebop Dominant 22
    D Bebop Major 22
    D Bebop Minor 22
    D Chinese 22
    D Dorian 22
    D Egyptian 23
    D Enigmatic 23
    D Gypsy 23
    D Harmonic Minor 23
    D Hindu 23
    D Hirajoshi 23
    D Hungarian 23
    D Japanese 23
    D Locrian 24
    D Lydian 24
    D Major Blues 24
    D Major (Ionian) 24
    D Melodic Minor 24
    D Minor Blues 24
    D Mixolydian 24
    D Nine Tone 24
    D Oriental 25
    D Pentatonic Major 25
    D Pentatonic Minor 25
    D Persian 25
    D Phrygian 25
    D Romanian Minor 25
    D Spanish 8 Tone 25
    D Spanish Gypsy 25
    D Symmetric Dim. 1 26
    D Symmetric Dim. 2 26
Root note: D♯/E♭ 26
    D♯/E♭ Aeolian 26
    D♯/E♭ Algerian 26
    D♯/E♭ Arabic 26
    D♯/E♭ Bebop Dominant 26
    D♯/E♭ Bebop Major 27
    D♯/E♭ Bebop Minor 27
    D♯/E♭ Chinese 27
    D♯/E♭ Dorian 27
    D♯/E♭ Egyptian 27
    D♯/E♭ Enigmatic 27
    D♯/E♭ Gypsy 27
    D♯/E♭ Harmonic Minor 27
    D♯/E♭ Hindu 28
    D♯/E♭ Hirajoshi 28
    D♯/E♭ Hungarian 28
    D♯/E♭ Japanese 28
    D♯/E♭ Locrian 28
    D♯/E♭ Lydian 28

4

D♯/E♭ Major Blues 28
D♯/E♭ Major (Ionian) 28
D♯/E♭ Melodic Minor 29
D♯/E♭ Minor Blues 29
D♯/E♭ Mixolydian 29
D♯/E♭ Nine Tone 29
D♯/E♭ Oriental 29
D♯/E♭ Pentatonic Major 29
D♯/E♭ Pentatonic Minor 29
D♯/E♭ Persian 29
D♯/E♭ Phrygian 30
D♯/E♭ Romanian Minor 30
D♯/E♭ Spanish 8 Tone 30
D♯/E♭ Spanish Gypsy 30
D♯/E♭ Symmetric Dim. 1 30
D♯/E♭ Symmetric Dim. 2 30
Root note: E 30
E Aeolian 31
E Algerian 31
E Arabic 31
E Bebop Dominant 31
E Bebop Major 31
E Bebop Minor 31
E Chinese 31
E Dorian 31
E Egyptian 32
E Enigmatic 32
E Gypsy 32
E Harmonic Minor 32
E Hindu 32
E Hirajoshi 32
E Hungarian 32
E Japanese 32
E Locrian 33
E Lydian 33
E Major Blues 33
E Major (Ionian) 33
E Melodic Minor 33
E Minor Blues 33
E Mixolydian 33
E Nine Tone 33
E Oriental 34
E Pentatonic Major 34
E Pentatonic Minor 34
E Persian 34
E Phrygian 34
E Romanian Minor 34
E Spanish 8 Tone 34
E Spanish Gypsy 34
E Symmetric Dim. 1 35
E Symmetric Dim. 2 35
Root note: F 35
F Aeolian 35
F Algerian 35
F Arabic 35
F Bebop Dominant 35
F Bebop Major 36
F Bebop Minor 36
F Chinese 36
F Dorian 36
F Egyptian 36
F Enigmatic 36
F Gypsy 36
F Harmonic Minor 36
F Hindu 37
F Hirajoshi 37
F Hungarian 37
F Japanese 37
F Locrian 37
F Lydian 37
F Major Blues 37
F Major (Ionian) 37

F Melodic Minor 38
F Minor Blues 38
F Mixolydian 38
F Nine Tone 38
F Oriental 38
F Pentatonic Major 38
F Pentatonic Minor 38
F Persian 38
F Phrygian 39
F Romanian Minor 39
F Spanish 8 Tone 39
F Spanish Gypsy 39
F Symmetric Dim. 1 39
F Symmetric Dim. 2 39
Root note: F♯/G♭ 39
F♯/G♭ Aeolian 40
F♯/G♭ Algerian 40
F♯/G♭ Arabic 40
F♯/G♭ Bebop Dominant 40
F♯/G♭ Bebop Major 40
F♯/G♭ Bebop Minor 40
F♯/G♭ Chinese 40
F♯/G♭ Dorian 40
F♯/G♭ Egyptian 41
F♯/G♭ Enigmatic 41
F♯/G♭ Gypsy 41
F♯/G♭ Harmonic Minor 41
F♯/G♭ Hindu 41
F♯/G♭ Hirajoshi 41
F♯/G♭ Hungarian 41
F♯/G♭ Japanese 41
F♯/G♭ Locrian 42
F♯/G♭ Lydian 42
F♯/G♭ Major Blues 42
F♯/G♭ Major (Ionian) 42
F♯/G♭ Melodic Minor 42
F♯/G♭ Minor Blues 42
F♯/G♭ Mixolydian 42
F♯/G♭ Nine Tone 42
F♯/G♭ Oriental 43
F♯/G♭ Pentatonic Major 43
F♯/G♭ Pentatonic Minor 43
F♯/G♭ Persian 43
F♯/G♭ Phrygian 43
F♯/G♭ Romanian Minor 43
F♯/G♭ Spanish 8 Tone 43
F♯/G♭ Spanish Gypsy 43
F♯/G♭ Symmetric Dim. 1 44
F♯/G♭ Symmetric Dim. 2 44
Root note: G 44
G Aeolian 44
G Algerian 44
G Arabic 44
G Bebop Dominant 44
G Bebop Major 45
G Bebop Minor 45
G Chinese 45
G Dorian 45
G Egyptian 45
G Enigmatic 45
G Gypsy 45
G Harmonic Minor 45
G Hindu 46
G Hirajoshi 46
G Hungarian 46
G Japanese 46
G Locrian 46
G Lydian 46
G Major Blues 46
G Major (Ionian) 46
G Melodic Minor 47
G Minor Blues 47

G Mixolydian 47
G Nine Tone 47
G Oriental 47
G Pentatonic Major 47
G Pentatonic Minor 47
G Persian 47
G Phrygian 48
G Romanian Minor 48
G Spanish 8 Tone 48
G Spanish Gypsy 48
G Symmetric Dim. 1 48
G Symmetric Dim. 2 48
Root note: G♯/A♭ 48
G♯/A♭ Aeolian 49
G♯/A♭ Algerian 49
G♯/A♭ Arabic 49
G♯/A♭ Bebop Dominant 49
G♯/A♭ Bebop Major 49
G♯/A♭ Bebop Minor 49
G♯/A♭ Chinese 49
G♯/A♭ Dorian 49
G♯/A♭ Egyptian 50
G♯/A♭ Enigmatic 50
G♯/A♭ Gypsy 50
G♯/A♭ Harmonic Minor 50
G♯/A♭ Hindu 50
G♯/A♭ Hirajoshi 50
G♯/A♭ Hungarian 50
G♯/A♭ Japanese 50
G♯/A♭ Locrian 51
G♯/A♭ Lydian 51
G♯/A♭ Major Blues 51
G♯/A♭ Major (Ionian) 51
G♯/A♭ Melodic Minor 51
G♯/A♭ Minor Blues 51
G♯/A♭ Mixolydian 51
G♯/A♭ Nine Tone 51
G♯/A♭ Oriental 52
G♯/A♭ Pentatonic Major 52
G♯/A♭ Pentatonic Minor 52
G♯/A♭ Persian 52
G♯/A♭ Phrygian 52
G♯/A♭ Romanian Minor 52
G♯/A♭ Spanish 8 Tone 52
G♯/A♭ Spanish Gypsy 52
G♯/A♭ Symmetric Dim. 1 53
G♯/A♭ Symmetric Dim. 2 53
Root note: A 53
A Aeolian 53
A Algerian 53
A Arabic 53
A Bebop Dominant 53
A Bebop Major 54
A Bebop Minor 54
A Chinese 54
A Dorian 54
A Egyptian 54
A Enigmatic 54
A Gypsy 54
A Harmonic Minor 54
A Hindu 55
A Hirajoshi 55
A Hungarian 55
A Japanese 55
A Locrian 55
A Lydian 55
A Major Blues 55
A Major (Ionian) 55
A Melodic Minor 56
A Minor Blues 56
A Mixolydian 56
A Nine Tone 56

A Oriental 56
A Pentatonic Major 56
A Pentatonic Minor 56
A Persian 56
A Phrygian 57
A Romanian Minor 57
A Spanish 8 Tone 57
A Spanish Gypsy 57
A Symmetric Dim. 1 57
A Symmetric Dim. 2 57
Root note: A♯/B♭ 57
A♯/B♭ Aeolian 58
A♯/B♭ Algerian 58
A♯/B♭ Arabic 58
A♯/B♭ Bebop Dominant 58
A♯/B♭ Bebop Major 58
A♯/B♭ Bebop Minor 58
A♯/B♭ Chinese 58
A♯/B♭ Dorian 58
A♯/B♭ Egyptian 59
A♯/B♭ Enigmatic 59
A♯/B♭ Gypsy 59
A♯/B♭ Harmonic Minor 59
A♯/B♭ Hindu 59
A♯/B♭ Hirajoshi 59
A♯/B♭ Hungarian 59
A♯/B♭ Japanese 59
A♯/B♭ Locrian 60
A♯/B♭ Lydian 60
A♯/B♭ Major Blues 60
A♯/B♭ Major (Ionian) 60
A♯/B♭ Melodic Minor 60
A♯/B♭ Minor Blues 60
A♯/B♭ Mixolydian 60
A♯/B♭ Nine Tone 60
A♯/B♭ Oriental 61
A♯/B♭ Pentatonic Major 61
A♯/B♭ Pentatonic Minor 61
A♯/B♭ Persian 61
A♯/B♭ Phrygian 61
A♯/B♭ Romanian Minor 61
A♯/B♭ Spanish 8 Tone 61
A♯/B♭ Spanish Gypsy 61
A♯/B♭ Symmetric Dim. 1 62
A♯/B♭ Symmetric Dim. 2 62
Root note: B 62
B Aeolian 62
B Algerian 62
B Arabic 62
B Bebop Dominant 62
B Bebop Major 63
B Bebop Minor 63
B Chinese 63
B Dorian 63
B Egyptian 63
B Enigmatic 63
B Gypsy 63
B Harmonic Minor 63
B Hindu 64
B Hirajoshi 64
B Hungarian 64
B Japanese 64
B Locrian 64
B Lydian 64
B Major Blues 64
B Major (Ionian) 64
B Melodic Minor 65
B Minor Blues 65
B Mixolydian 65
B Nine Tone 65
B Oriental 65
B Pentatonic Major 65

B Pentatonic Minor 65
B Persian 65
B Phrygian 66
B Romanian Minor 66
B Spanish 8 Tone 66
B Spanish Gypsy 66
B Symmetric Dim. 1 66
B Symmetric Dim. 2 66
Movable 'Box' Scale Patterns 67
Aeolian 67
Algerian 67
Arabic 67
Bebop Dominant 68
Bebop Major 68
Bebop Minor 68
Chinese 68
Dorian 69
Egyptian 69
Enigmatic 69
Gypsy 69
Harmonic Minor 70
Hindu 70
Hirajoshi 70
Hungarian 70
Japanese 71
Locrian 71
Lydian 71
Major Blues 71
Major (Ionian) 72
Melodic Minor 72
Minor Blues 72
Mixolydian 72
Nine Tone 73
Oriental 73
Pentatonic Major 73
Pentatonic Minor 73
Persian 74
Phrygian 74
Romanian Minor 74
Spanish 8 Tone 74
Spanish Gypsy 75
Symmetric Dim. 1 75
Symmetric Dim. 2 75

The Aims of This Book

"I promise if you work on scales for two hours a day for two years, you will become a fine [cellist / insert instrument of your choice?]. I keep my promises." Hans 'Enke' Zentgraf.

The aim of this book is not to present you with a method for learning your scales faster. Like Hans Zentgraf, I do not believe the road to becoming a better musician can be navigated at great speed. For the average person with other things to be done during the day, two hours per day on scales practise alone[1] represents **a lot of work** and moreover, **commitment**, right? The way to learn your scales faster is by practising them more often, in greater variety and over the full range of positions on the fingerboard.

This book will provide you with the raw ingredients to help you to learn a wide variety of scales and modes, it is up to you to put in the work to learn these scales and to learn how to use them effectively in context. Everybody learns differently and (thankfully) plays differently; with this book, the information you need to master a scale is at your fingertips.

I wish you the best of luck and, most importantly, enjoyment in the **process** of learning.

Why Learn to Play Scales?

Learning to play a variety of scales makes you a better musician. **It teaches your fingers** where to find and how to handle the different positions you might encounter when playing pieces of music, **it trains your musical ear** by helping you to learn to recognise intervals and how they relate to finger positioning, and ultimately **it trains your musical brain** how to recognise different musical colours and eventually create them on the fly.

How to Use This Book

A picture is worth a thousand words.

Figure 1:   Example figure showing the position of the notes of the C major scale.

The primary purpose of this book is to help you visualise the locations of the notes of a scale on the mandolin fingerboard, a typical diagram in the book is shown in Figure 1. This particular page gives you information about the C Major scale. It shows the position of the notes of the C Major scale up to the position on the fingerboard 17 semitones above the nut.

---

[1] Note that scales practise should form only part of your practise regime.

On the **left hand side of the diagram**, you will see numbers from 0 (the nut) to 17: these represent the number of semitones above the nut each horizontal line corresponds to. On a fretted instrument, the **horizontal lines** would correspond to frets, but if you have bought this book for use with an instrument without frets or fret markings, then you need to use your mind's eye to visualise these positions (doing so is an excellent mental exercise). The diagrams are scaled so that the location of the horizontal lines is in proportion to where they would appear on a real instrument, this will help you see visually and thus anticipate physically the contraction in finger spacing required in moving the scale further up the neck of the instrument. The large **solid dots** in the main diagram show the locations of the notes of the scale in question. **Ringed dots** show the location of the root notes of the scale. Also provided with each fingerboard diagram are the notes in score notation and the defining intervals of each scale, which follow the key given in Table 1. For example, the Ionian mode (or major scale) would be notated: T T S T T T S.

Using Scale Diagrams to Construct Exercises

Exactly in which order you need to play the notes of a given scale over a given number of octaves I leave to you, the reader. This is part of the purpose of this book – to give you ideas about the various ways you could finger a scale, or musical phrase. The movable box scales can be used to see how a scale might be played in a particular position on the neck. The full fingerboard diagrams can be used to see how these box patterns can be connected together, or to help you develop your own scale fingerings, which might include shifts.

Notation	Interval
S	Semitone / Augmented unison
T	Tone / Major 2nd
m3	Minor 3rd
M3	Major 3rd
p4	Perfect 4th
d5	Diminished 5th
p5	Perfect 5th
m6	Minor 6th
M6	Major 6th
m7	Minor 7th
M7	Major 7th

Table 1: Key to interval notation.

Typical exercises you could develop include:

- playing the scale over a given number of octaves in ascending and then descending order;

- playing the scale in sequences e.g. if '1' and '2' denote the first and second notes of the scale etc. then the sequences 1,2,3, 2,3,4, 3,4,5, 4,5,6, 5,6,7 ,6,7,8, 8,7,6, 7,6,5, 6,5,4, 5,4,3, 4,3,2, 3,2,1 or 1,2,3,1, 2,3,4,2, 3,4,5,3, 4,5,6,4 etc. might provide a good starting point;

- playing the scale and skipping over some notes e.g. using the notation above: 1,3,5,7,8,6,4,2;

- using a background drone note set to the pitch of the root note of the scale, experiment by improvising phrases, or executing scale sequences to see how they sound in context.

The possibilities are endless! My advice would be to construct sequences based around the scale patterns you are trying to learn that appear in real pieces of music. You should also add variation to your practising of scales by changing the timing of notes (e.g. playing them at an even tempo, in triplets, sixteenths, or with a galloping or syncopated rhythm), and phrasing (e.g. emphasising distinct notes, or slurring, or a combination). Recall that for the melodic minor scale (a.k.a. 'Jazz Minor'), the notes ascending and descending are different.

Author's Notes on this Edition

To avoid over-cluttering the diagrams, I have not included the names of the notes (or scale degrees) on the fingerboard diagrams. I have, however, included for each scale the notes in score notation. In all cases, I have elected to use sharps to indicate accidentals. The reason for this is that these scales could appear in any key and technically, the precise choice of accidentals as a combination of sharps and/or flats would be determined by the key of the piece at the point the notes appeared in the music. To present all possible enharmonic equivalents would not be an efficient use of space.

I welcome **constructive** feedback on my book. Please feel free to contact me with comments by email using the address benjamin.cello.mad.taylor@googlemail.com. In particular, if you would like a scales or arpeggios book, for a stringed instrument in an unusual tuning, please don't hesitate to let me know.

C♯/D♭ Hindu

T T S T S T T

C♯/D♭ Hirajoshi

S M3 S M3 T

C♯/D♭ Hungarian

T S m3 S S m3 S

C♯/D♭ Japanese

S M3 T m3 T

C♯/D♭ Locrian

S T T S T T T

C♯/D♭ Lydian

T T T S T T S

C♯/D♭ Major Blues

T S S m3 T m3

C♯/D♭ Major (Ionian)

T T S T T T S

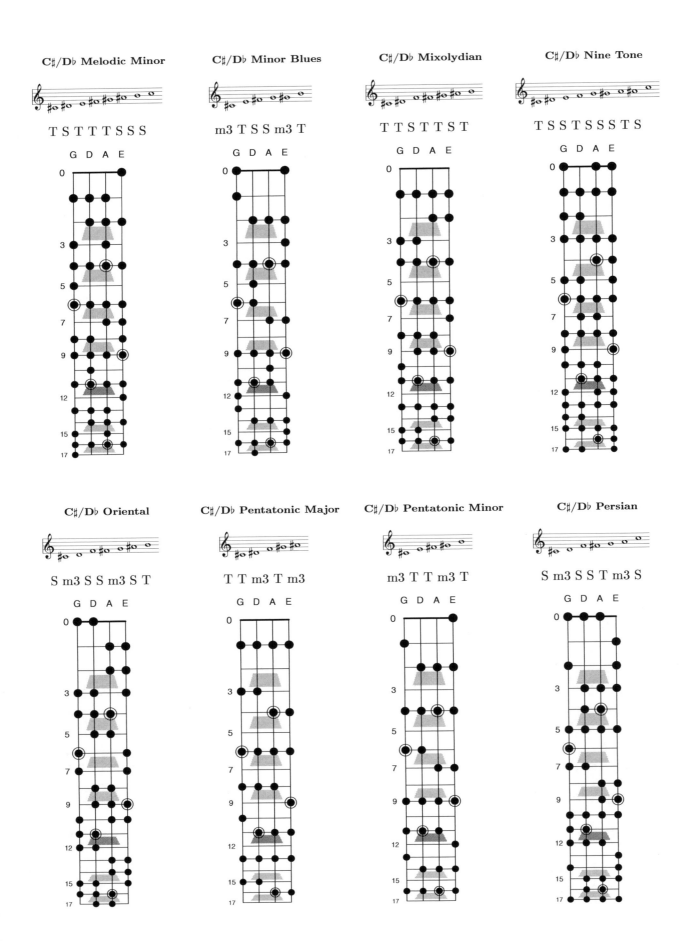

C♯/D♭ Phrygian

S T T T S T T

C♯/D♭ Romanian Minor

T S m3 S T S T

C♯/D♭ Spanish 8 Tone

S T S S S T T T

C♯/D♭ Spanish Gypsy

S m3 S T S T T

C♯/D♭ Symmetric Dim. 1

S T S T S T S T

C♯/D♭ Symmetric Dim. 2

T S T S T S T S

D Locrian

S T T S T T T

D Lydian

T T T S T T S

D Major Blues

T S S m3 T m3

D Major (Ionian)

T T S T T T S

D Melodic Minor

T S T T T S S S

D Minor Blues

m3 T S S m3 T

D Mixolydian

T T S T T S T

D Nine Tone

T S S T S S S T S

24

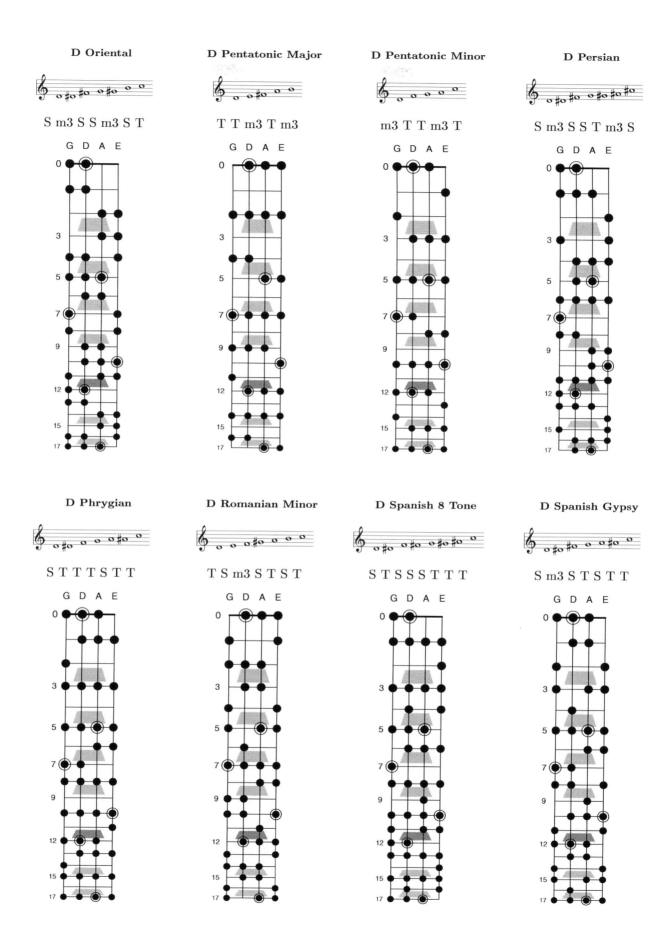

D Symmetric Dim. 1

S T S T S T S T

D Symmetric Dim. 2

T S T S T S T S

D♯/E♭ Aeolian

T S T T S T T

D♯/E♭ Algerian

T S T S S S m3 S

D♯/E♭ Arabic

T T S S T T T

D♯/E♭ Bebop Dominant

T T S T T S S S

26

D♯/E♭ Phrygian

S T T T S T T

D♯/E♭ Romanian Minor

T S m3 S T S T

D♯/E♭ Spanish 8 Tone

S T S S S T T T

D♯/E♭ Spanish Gypsy

S m3 S T S T T

D♯/E♭ Symmetric Dim. 1

S T S T S T S T

D♯/E♭ Symmetric Dim. 2

T S T S T S T S

F Phrygian

STTTSTT

F Romanian Minor

T S m3 S T S T

F Spanish 8 Tone

STSSSTTT

F Spanish Gypsy

S m3 S T S T T

F Symmetric Dim. 1

STSTSTST

F Symmetric Dim. 2

TSTSTSTS

41

F♯/G♭ Symmetric Dim. 1   **F♯/G♭ Symmetric Dim. 2**

S T S T S T S T   T S T S T S T S

G Aeolian   **G Algerian**   **G Arabic**   **G Bebop Dominant**

T S T T S T T   T S T S S S m3 S   T T S S T T T   T T S T T S S S

G Phrygian **G Romanian Minor** **G Spanish 8 Tone** **G Spanish Gypsy**

S T T T S T T   T S m3 S T S T   S T S S S T T T   S m3 S T S T T

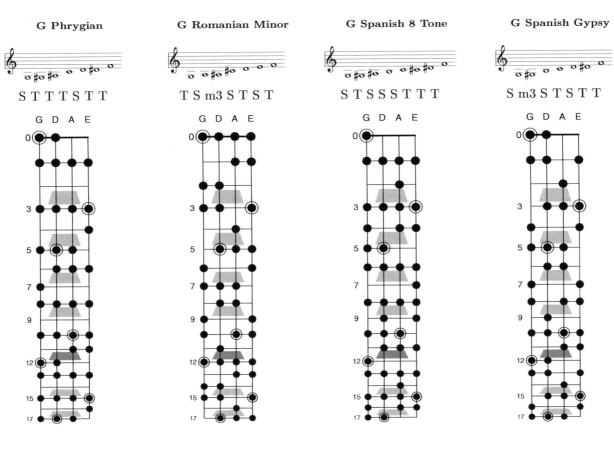

G Symmetric Dim. 1 **G Symmetric Dim. 2**

S T S T S T S T   T S T S T S T S

G♯/A♭ Symmetric Dim. 1   **G♯/A♭ Symmetric Dim. 2**

STSTSTST   TSTSTSTS

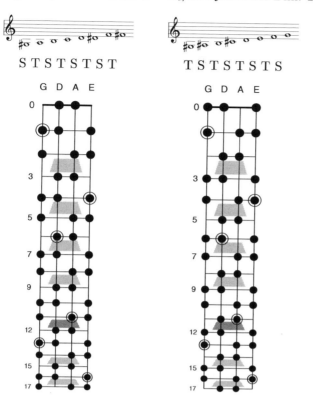

A Aeolian   **A Algerian**   **A Arabic**   **A Bebop Dominant**

TSTTSTT   TSTSSS m3 S   TTSSTTT   TTSTTSSS

A Phrygian

S T T T S T T

A Romanian Minor

T S m3 S T S T

A Spanish 8 Tone

S T S S S T T T

A Spanish Gypsy

S m3 S T S T T

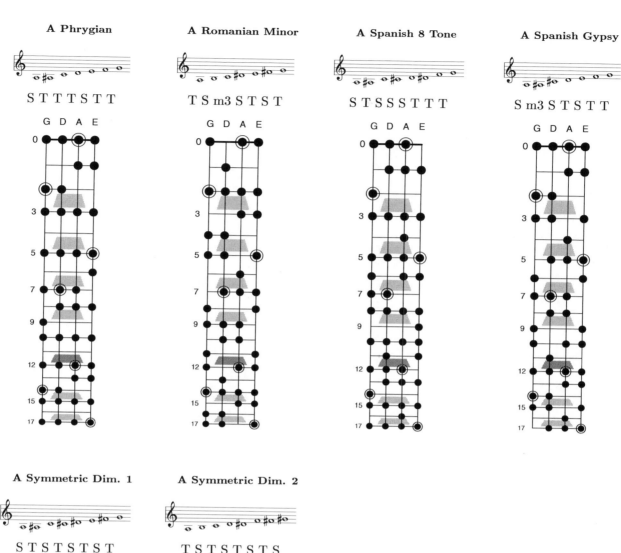

A Symmetric Dim. 1

S T S T S T S T

A Symmetric Dim. 2

T S T S T S T S

A♯/B♭ Symmetric Dim. 1

S T S T S T S T

A♯/B♭ Symmetric Dim. 2

T S T S T S T S

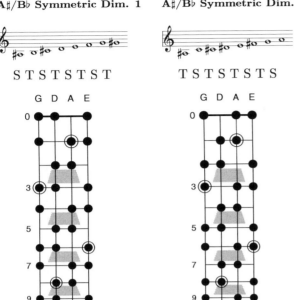

B Aeolian

T S T T S T T

B Algerian

T S T S S S m3 S

B Arabic

T T S S T T T

B Bebop Dominant

T T S T T S S S

Melodic Minor

T S T T T S S S

B Minor Blues

m3 T S S m3 T

B Mixolydian

T T S T T S T

B Nine Tone

T S S T S S S T S

B Oriental

S m3 S S m3 S T

B Pentatonic Major

T T m3 T m3

B Pentatonic Minor

m3 T T m3 T

B Persian

S m3 S S T m3 S

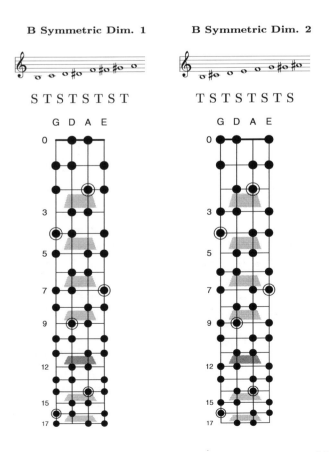

Movable 'Box' Scale Patterns

Aeolian

Algerian

Arabic

Bebop Dominant

Bebop Major

Bebop Minor

Chinese

Dorian

Egyptian

Enigmatic

Gypsy

Harmonic Minor

Hindu

Hirajoshi

Hungarian

Japanese

Locrian

Lydian

Major Blues

Major (Ionian)

Melodic Minor

Minor Blues

Mixolydian

Nine Tone

Oriental

Pentatonic Major

Pentatonic Minor

Persian

Phrygian

Romanian Minor

Spanish 8 Tone

Spanish Gypsy

Symmetric Dim. 1

Symmetric Dim. 2

Made in the USA
Middletown, DE
17 July 2017